BIG FIRE AT SPAHN RANCH

BIG FIRE AT SPAHN RANCH

RICHARD ARTHUR BOWERING, JR.

Great Horned Publishing

Book design and typesetting by Ron Jost
Cover design and hand lettering by Tim Lokiec
Cover image copyright © Tim Lokiec

First Edition
First Printing: Summer 2011

Printed in the United States of America

ISBN: 978-0-578-06160-3

GreatHornedPublishing.com

To those people both real and imagined
who are trapped between these covers.

Contents

PART I

Katie   3

Richard Chase at the Navajo Shopping Center   4

Shorty's Last Stand   5

And Then the Song Conjured Up Your Soft White Shoulders
     All Over Again   6

Fenway Park at Season's End: Wally the Green Monster   7

On Punching My House (A Soliloquy)   9

In This Dream, I Turn Around and Find My Father's Grandfather
     Alive Again   10

Remnant   11

Snow-Man   12

Late Autumn, Raymond   14

The Wild Woman Chase of 1878   15

The Gods Fabricate Misfortunes So That Future Generations
     Will Have Something to Sing About   17

Waiter   19

There's a Stranger Inside the Gate   21

PART II

Celmer Goes AWOL   25

Memoirs of an Aesthete   26

At Versace's   27

Snipers Crawl from Chevy Caprice Trunks and
      Suburban Living Rooms   28

The Dogmatics   30

Death Comes to the Kid   31

Closing Salvo   32

We're The Del Crandalls, Parts II and III (A Four-Part,
      Ten-Year Special Commemorative Set. Collect All Four!)   34

You Have Killed Sweet Love's Groovy Stance   35

To the homeboy who stole my car stereo with tape 3, side 2
      from "A Century of Recorded Poetry" still in it
      (on the occasion of Richard Eberhart's 99th birthday)   36

A Real Homey Tragedy   38

Raymond, Maine   39

Resurrection of the Packard Tribe   40

Deal to the Class—   41

Returns   42

Traits: Sixteen Stones in a Field   44

PART III

Fall   47

Fort Nathan Hale Death Stanzas   48

Winter Piss, Outside the Shock-Ward   49

Still Life with Marriage Counselor   50

Symphony for Pond Mud, Several Gifted Frogs, and the Death
      of the Last Survivor of the Spanish Inquisition   52

A Dinner Bell Unanswered   53

St. Brigid and the Gull Who Would Be a Man   54

TV Baby   56

The Crows   57

This Skull Once Had a Tongue   58

THE DEL CRANDALLS *(Song Lyrics)*

Tex   61

Common Man   63

Two Days of Rain   64

Rye Beach Roustabouts   65

Our Town   66

Man Ray   67

Ginger Snaps   68

Acknowledgements   69

About the Author   70

PART I

Katie

*Just as I caught up to Abigail Folger and raised my arm up to
stab her, some little voice inside me said "this is wrong." But it
was too late to stop. And then I saw Tex coming to finish the job.*

– Former Manson Family member Patricia "Katie"
Krenwinkel in jailhouse interview with Diane Sawyer

I flew through French doors streaked and splattered with blood
And across the lawn. The steak knife stretched over my head
As if it would scrape the arc of sky.

Stars shook out over the blackness. Abigail Folger,
Exhausted and beyond words, tripped
On her nightgown. Over and over my knife sunk, deep,

Hitting bone. The cold air rushed against my teeth.
My arm, still small and ladylike, bashing this girl insensate,

Froze over her in mid-plunge as Tex roared up,
A gleaming, pulsing monster, to rip at her heart.
And something spoke in my heart then.

Her pretty eyes drifted. The sad, intimate pool of her blood
Gave back my face, stuck in a wild rash of stars.

Richard Chase at the Navajo Shopping Center

Richard Chase was the obsessive "Vampire of Sacramento."
After roaming the country for a year, he went on a murder spree,
drinking his victims' blood. He was caught and locked up in a
mental hospital, where he would somehow grab birds that lived
in the hospital's patio area, break their necks, and then at night
secretly leave them, two at a time, neatly outside the doors of the
other patients' rooms.

Alfalfa for sale in small square bales:
Dry, fine stemmed, leafy.
Wire-tied, stored in barns.
No stickers.

Quality Orchardgrass and straw, from clean fields and bug free.
Prairie and Blue Tick hay in wire or plastic twine.

Five hundred bales of good Kentucky Bluegrass
With high protein content for feeding wildlife.
Bright horse hay. No rain on any of it.
A hundred-fifty bales to feed goats.
A semi-load of cow hay to haul.

Alfalfa, wheat, timothy-orchard grass —

I do not remember exactly when I knew
For the first time
That I could see inside the minds of birds.

Shorty's Last Stand

But the one she liked best, she said, was Clem.
Clem with the idiot grin.
Clem, who chopped Shorty Shea's head off with a shovel . . .

– From *Helter Skelter* by Vincent Bugliosi

Shorty Shea was hiking down to the canyon that morning, she told me, *with Clem and Tex, some of the others. Perhaps Charlie. Definitely Charlie. It was starting to get cold out. I got up and burned the bag with the coins in it, then Sadie gave me some acid and I went back to sleep. Katie and Linda had gone up the hill with their babies. They said they saw some birds up there, but the birds had the faces of some people they knew, so they came back down and made breakfast. I heard a scream; I couldn't tell if it was a guy or a girl or a jackal. It woke me up, and I smelled the purse burning, even though the fire was out by then. Tex came back to my room later and told me to hide his gun. His eyes were dead and glowy like Susan said they were up at the Tate house. He told me to hide his gun in my room somewhere. The vibrations began to get really weird. I thought about my mother back in Ventura County. Tex told me he was a Methodist and that meant he was very orderly. While we were fucking on the bed, Clem came in with the shovel. The bottom was wet and red. This was because he had used it to cut Shorty's head off. Clem was smiling. He sniffed at the window and started singing some song, I think it was "The Shadow of Your Smile." We all smelled the coin purse burning, but Clem said it's not the purse burning, stupid, it's Shorty crackling and bubbling out in Devil's Canyon. Then Charlie's face was in my window; he looked like Jesus or something. He held up Shorty's guns, laughed, and shot them in the air. Clem started spinning around and laughing. That's when I started to think about getting the hell out of there.* I left her alone in the interrogation room and went to the phone to notify Shea's parents. I looked back. She was playing with a strand of her hair. After the call, I went into the locker room. I took my head into my hands and I cried. Later on, a fire spread all down the canyon. It wiped out 900 acres, including the Spahn Cowboy Movie Ranch. Even though Charlie was in San Quentin, the fire just kept on spreading.

And Then the Song Conjured Up Your Soft White Shoulders All Over Again

I shuffle home under a midnight sky.
Blinking neon bothers smoking cousins
Drunk and distracted with braggadocio. Dozens
Of scratchy violins lift from a tenement door nearby:

I poke my head inside. An old man in a pork-pie hat
Listens to Sinatra's "September of My Years."
He's in Frank's world, where it's always 1954:
V-8 sedans purr to the curb,
Two-olive V.O. martinis are shaken extra dry,
Jilly Rizzo does in the goons at the Copa.

But the Manhattan jazz in this joint
Of a world gets loud fast, so I call out
Hey Big Chief, I gotta go and split to a swelling of hot brass
While an ambulance somewhere shrieks *nothing matters at all.*

And long into the night I think about how I would love to kiss you
As the lights go out, as your gown and hair lazily fall.

Fenway Park at Season's End: Wally the Green Monster

October. Wally lights a cigarette,
Takes a long drag, stares at the glowing tip.
Sits somewhere in Section 42. It's quiet.

He can still hear his mother's shrill yap:
Don't have babies with people.
But he did, and that night of unprotected sex

Produced little Jimmy, with greenish skin, who
Hangs his big square head as he walks down the hallway at school,
Half-boy half-mascot. The shotgun marriage was over

In six months – a freak for mascots, she left Wally for
Dave, the Self-Denying Fish. Finally settled for (of course)
The Fightin' Mule, encountered outside a porn trade show.

Jimmy doesn't want to learn the trade.
But what else will he do? *Same attitude as Lobster-Boy's kid.*
Flicking his Lucky Strike, Wally swallows the last of his
Jack Daniels and, groping down the concourse to piss,

Stops to hose down a wall. No matter.
Later on, he stumbles across center field, and words bear down
On him like a necklace of tires: *Divorced. Absent father. Clown.*

Wally knows that mascots are really just rowdy tourists
In the human world, covered with the foreign dust of ball fields:
Green and fuzzy! Spouting macabre caricatures of human heads,
And grotesque limbs! Flashing huge animal claws and teeth!

———

7

Looking up at the scoreboard before entering the secret door
And going to bed for the winter, he whips a crowd of pigeons
Into a great frenzy. One day his son will look in the mirror and see

Behind his own green head the shadows of a thousand human faces
Waiting for his cue. He will hear in that moment the roar that signifies
Both icon life and icon death.

On Punching My House (A Soliloquy)

Nursing my purple wrist, I wonder:
Knuckle marks fisted around the door moldings
And by the railing, under thickest paint.

Who made them?

The near barn settles, no longer protecting completely
The dull, cold mews of heavy hay,
The scattered bones of livestock lifted off the scales
Of a long-forgotten market day
Or the ghosts of hard men – the Southworths,
Arthur Bangs, Colonel Bronson –
Who once, like me, lived in the house
And found silence in that barn,
A place to smoke, drink whisky, and cradle
The tender result of uncontrolled fist on clapboard.

These long nights, the barn cowers under winter's harsh darkness.
For miles the town hangs heavy, like wet pine.
Freshly slugged, my house sags under another winter.
The barn sees it all.

Drunk, I move through the shadows
Hoping nobody sees this pig who has freed himself from under the gate.

In This Dream, I Turn Around and Find
My Father's Grandfather Alive Again

I.

I'll return again to Uncanoonuc:
A mound of rotted boards, willy-nilly,
Collapsed over a solid slab foundation,
Like an old drunk down for a post-coital snooze.

The foundation can't push it off, *resquiat en pax,*
So the silent battle continues,
Neither giving in, board side or stone side.
A broad carpet of maple leaves hides the flattened shed.

Trees grow straight through soft
Knot-holes and breaks in wood slab.
The rusted hulk of an Apperson Jackrabbit crouches
On the hill, haven for bees and newts.

The hearth rises semi-erect from the center,
Giving out in broad, man-struck eructions of local granite.
The fireplace faces east, half-sunk in loam,
Home to starlings and blue finches and a rotted hickory flail.

II.

I come back to this small pass again in a dream,
My head dizzy with of out-of-town words.

Within, the sound of a motor leaping to life
As the old man limps from the barn.

Remnant

*In 1864, Rev. E. B. Hillard set out to find and photograph the
last living soldiers of the American Revolution.*

One hundred four years old, he sits for the camera man
Half-alive, marbles for eyes, vacant.
Gums no more incisive than a baby's flop inside a span of white beard.
Propped in a hand-lathed Allegheny ploughman's chair
Smelling like hickory smoke and dry leather among his obedient animals.
It's December. His mind is gone over the hills
With the flakes traveling through the sky.

Conscripted into the 7th Pennsylvania Militia at thirteen,
He shouldered up to hot-livered men who bore the yoke of the powder-cart,
Screwing the hod and the flail for the grimness of duty.
He took small drilling in the camp but soon stepped, lost,
Through the woods and fields of his Pennsylvania. He once said
After I lost my gun, I carried only a stick.
I went days without seeing another person.

The stones stand cold, moss freezes like chaff.
The forest around the churchyard cracks with a hundred trees.

One loose, palsied fist can't hold anything, not even the memory of
    a boy with a stick.

Snow-Man

Pratt's funeral parlor spills somber men in worsted suits
Past Devil's Brook and over the Killingworth Road.
The freezing rain sends hunched dark ladies in veils
Flying down the walk.
That water raises flowers.
The small drowned skater stays, folded in his box.

Over here by the sugar maples, hickory-stuck, snow-headed,
Propped near the bog in a bank of snow,
I tilt in my place below the hill.

Battered by northern squalls and now icy rain.
Stump of a pipe stuck in my frozen cannon ball head,
Mitten-compacted, erected and wholly forgotten.
Stovepipe hat blown into the woods, carrot for a nose,
Raisin eyes washed away, sticks for arms,
Sunk alone at the bottom of the hill.

I know the delicate conversation of icy brook and cattails,
The hushed world of the bog. Rains harden my body, frozen.
I watch the chimneys of three little houses as they harden into sleep.
A blackbird stirs under a bush. The moan of a lone sow splayed
In the stiff muck spills out over the field and is endless.

Now come the dark small steps of children in flight. In mittens and scarves,
They leave one behind at the funeral parlor, the one who sang,
    who played with them
In nights of fireflies, who heard those sounds over the bog-stream that march
Like slow-footed armies through tangled secret places
The moon won't enter. In the front window of the funeral home
Reposes the small ice-cracking brooder, silent and still in his tiny Sunday suit,
Harboring the mud-song and mask of dreamland. That water smashes life.

I am overcome: I too am waxing into a new phase, like
    the Hunchback phase of the moon.
The nights become shorter, but my mantle of night stays
A long time. There is something dark about me

That I will carry to my end.
But before the new sun cracks the world to rend my snowy life,
When they lay me straight out in the box, my witch hazel wrists
    bent unnaturally,

I want to know: will the dead boy's song rise up from the bog to take me?
Will God, wearing His finest mittens, fashion me a resurrection body of
    pure gold?

Late Autumn, Raymond

The night they found Plummer near the cherry grove
We heard it again: Indian trouble coming down.

He had left town over the footbridge.
Little Hattie Libby, in her fever,
Tells her mother this story:
Last night I saw his image
Flash strange signs from out on the lake,
From high water in a scow,
Between two ghost oarsmen.

The shadows at the oars skim Sebago on near-soundless skeins of light.
They sit backwards, half-lit by a small shielded candle.
Soon enough, Hattie Libby will ride between them lit a faint yellow,
Paler than the moon's face between November storm clouds,
As off the Notch, a mother howls the village unhallowed.

The Indian walks toe to heel.
Silent, like oars hung over hayricks.
He flies from bush to bush. Look. He's behind the cherry tree.

When death comes, we must all howl through the houses lakeward,
Lit by sheltered candles that explode in the night sky like cherry trees.

The Wild Woman Chase of 1878

She mixed sense with nonsense.
Sought out snakes and spiders.

She grew older and more in the way.
Her frequent absences became more
Extended, distal. Her returns, infrequent,

Were like the return of a bad animal:
The laugh, so unnatural for so long, became a sound

Out of nature. A warning sound. Some nights
The sound would bounce to the village from
The lake. Mothers would call their children in.

————

In the newspaper clipping from 1948,
Belle Harmon points to Frye's Island, where
The Wild Woman Chase of 1878 took place.

Eight years old when the baby was stolen,
She and her mother had started from the water tentative,
Holding hands with the hands of the
Village, encircling the small patch of land. The march to the

Center was met with desolation. The ring of faces,
Now close together, took on the hard look of loss.
A shout broke the meeting. They ran to the part

Where the big rotten log was. The fog had come down,
But you could make out a small dory. Two men in straw hats

Sat fore and aft. She sat in the center, all in black,
Covered in dirt. She was holding the baby. It looked dead.

————

In 1975 the shopping center went in. The island was
Connected with the shore for extra parking. Birds
Pick at things of interest by the curb. Car accidents happen
Infrequently on the Interstate. Clouds whip by like racing demons in the sky.

The Gods Fabricate Misfortunes So That Future Generations Will Have Something to Sing About

In a clearing, we saw the monk.
For years, he walked by the ocean
In a steady fit of madness
And all the babies in Ireland would rain howls down in his path.
One day, he banged together a small wooden boat.

He was mad about the ocean.
He was obsessed with poetry.
He was consumed by the howls.
He was drowning steadily, he was being yanked down.
He fought the processions of laughing demons.
He was a mad monk.

He was the *enfant terrible* of his order:
He would howl at night to the banshees.
He would obsess over elaborate poetic forms.
He found a bastard Irish baby.
The monk stole the baby.

The people in the south of Ireland,
When the baby was found missing,
Formed an angry, frantic procession.
They met at the ocean and joined hands.
Steady now, said a farmer.
May God stand up for the bastards.

The baby lay soiled in the boat.
The baby rode the ocean.
The baby became obsessed with the monk.
The baby howled steadily, from far out in the Irish Sea.
The baby began to speak.
The baby addressed the monk:

———

We will be watchers in the woods.
We will be swift to anger, and swift to retaliate.
We will know the course of the stars.
We will be leaders of men.
We will be masters of poetry.
We will lead processions of babies and monks on the oceans.

There will be a hot bath in our house, and a steady supply of beer.
There will be oceans of poetry. All the bastards in Ireland will be stolen by monks.
We will now proceed to the shore. We must tell those wailing farmers on the shore.

Waiter

Over at the bar,
Reading the racing form,
Half-eye, fixed and blue like a sturgeon's, on the clock.

Wee mustache marches along upper lip
Like a band of grenadiers.
An accident with a milk truck in your boyhood
Left that scar on your forehead,
Purple as a Union tank.

Once you were denied service here.
You went into the night swinging,
Your eyes wide plates of fish,
Two Atlantic Platter Specials.

Tonight at closing time you will zag past shut bars
To the firehouse for final round
Through a night blue like wool,
Mouth clamped on your smoke.

You'll return home when the newspaper trucks hit the streets,
An ancient, soused guerrilla grousing
About blood and waves and horses,
Calling out girl's names you wrote in the covers of schoolbooks.

In your dreams you rake through cities back home
In your pressed blue smock,
The Waiter. Catholic. An American.
Blue tin roofs and roofs of thatch appear and disappear.
You light on phone wires from Derry to Down.
You sing as you connect patterns of weather over the coiling surface of
    the sea.

———

The body retains little of this life, even bone, you think,
As the first crow of morning calls out *Laughing Boy*
And the blue wool of your city keens back:
Bastard, bastard, bastard.

There's a Stranger Inside the Gate

When your bone china-blue face emerged,
I felt drunk:
It wasn't the viscous, hairy red thing projected
In the Super-8s of the La Maze boot camp,
But an alabaster death mask: ancient, brittle.
Cast from a cherub's face on the parapet of Portsmouth Abbey.
Perfect.

Last Thanksgiving, I tried to picture you at our table next year. I couldn't.
Now here you were, wearing crisp baby clothes but somehow wild.
Still seeming to straddle two worlds. Ready for this one now.

For those first few months I felt like the brutish Gauls who,
After a long descent into darkness,
Crouched in terror and exhilaration
As St. Patrick and his small procession
Assembled inside the city gates
And shook the blackness to the ground.

PART II

Celmer Goes AWOL

We were in line for the roller coaster
When he decided to tell me about his five weeks in the Army:
I hated boot camp, the drill sergeants,
The close quarters, waking up at oh-four hundred hours.
But if I didn't get out of the house,
My father would have killed me.
He was hitting me with tools
And had started waving his gun around near us.

But soon the army too had started beating on him,
So he went AWOL:
I took off in the middle of the night
On a crazy route that took me through five states
East and west. Eight days later, two government agents
Found me somehow
In New York state, in the middle of nowhere,
And put me in the back of their car.

They didn't talk to me all the way back to South Carolina.
Nothing. They took me into a room when I got back to the base.
The Chaplain was there, and a couple of guards.

And then the Chaplain says:
"Sorry to hear about your father, Celmer. If you had told us,
We would certainly have allowed you to attend the funeral.
Under the circumstances, we have decided to give you a discharge
And to not press charges."

And that was how he learned of his father's heart attack:
See? The only nice thing that bastard ever did for me
Was to die at the right time.

The carnival grounds had turned ominous and dark,
And the Ferris wheel groaned in a big leering arc.

Memoirs of an Aesthete

The applause indicated a sort of agreement.
Our singers marched forward
Holding their costumes high over their heads in triumph,
And then it was my turn to ascend to the podium.

The strings and brass swelled and died down.
Thrusting a well-blown nose toward my admiring faithful,
I commenced. My speech was touching with
Humorous and sentimental flourishes.

After dismissing the ladies of our joyous troupe,
I went home and later that evening sat down with pen in hand
To begin a new and plainer version
Of the work which had so brilliantly launched my career,

A career that will take me far away
From the chores of a romantic existence.

At Versace's

This young man – who wears no makeup
And probably does not even moisturize his skin –
How are we to account for him,
And for his shocking presence upon the scene?

There is a rumor that he will not kiss –
Even when bullied –
And when he dances, there is no emotion:

He sways slowly to the music,
Clicking his fingers to the beat.

Snipers Crawl from Chevy Caprice Trunks and Suburban Living Rooms

Commando cops storm the rest stop on the I-70,
Find the Bushmaster .223-caliber rifle in the car,
Make the arrest in a highway raid:

Muhammad and Malvo
caught sleeping in a car.
[Malvo (left) with Muhammad in an undated photo.]

Rifle, scope, and tripod are dropped in an evidence bag,
The vehicle's impounded,
And soon it's on the radio:

Muhammad and Malvo
Caught sleeping in a car.
[Malvo (left) with Muhammad in an undated photo.]

The sniper task force,
A freeway rest stop before dawn,
A Gulf War veteran,
His 17-year-old stepson,
A Jamaican citizen.

Authorities made a match to a fingerprint
From a shooting at a liquor store.
There were some similarities to a composite sketch.

This is such a shock, a sister-in-law would say –
Nothing in their demeanor told us that
They were capable of any violent act,

And it was such a shock when you destroyed me:
Nothing in your demeanor told me that
You were capable of your violent attack on my heart

There were no fingerprints, no matches, no similarities to you
No composite sketch
You had me in your scope
Stormed in under cover of night

I was caught sleeping
[You (left) with me in an undated photo.]

The Dogmatics

We were in the Midwest somewhere, Indiana or somewhere, and some kids said to us "You talk funny." We said, no, we're from Boston, Massachusetts — you're the ones who talk funny.

– Paul O'Halloran, 1985

One night we went to see The Dogmatics at The Grotto. Their big song, "Sister Serena," was about a mean nun. Peter O'Halloran, the little guitar player, had a dirty plaster cast on up to his right thigh. I never found out why. He was perched leg-up in a lawn chair that was new, like it had just come from the store. His twin, Paul, careened around the stage playing bass, sometimes losing control on the turns. One afternoon two months later he lost control of his motorcycle and died on the Southeast Expressway.

Getting ready for tomorrow's tag sale, I sort through my record collection as the yard grows quiet. It's a million years later and I'm on the other side of the country. Night climbs down as I come across the only Dogmatics album: *Thayer Street,* from 1984. On the back cover is a phone number to call for "Information and updates about the band!" I dial, and a recording says the number doesn't exist.

Death Comes to the Kid

*Ted knew his daughter broke into his house and stole all those
awards so she could sell them for booze. Rather than call the
police, he drove north for his hunting trip, as planned.
"She needed them more than I did, I guess," he told me later.*

– From *Hitter: the Life and Turmoils of Ted Williams,* by
Ed Linn

On the day the girl came to bear the trophies away,
You were thirty miles outside Bangor.
You paddled east for a half hour,
Saw a buck. It paused, ate, wandered from your sights.

Now on this, your last afternoon,
From somewhere in your coma,
You heave the big Remington to your shoulder

As a black crow flies into the low hall of your memory:
Past shards of drunk broken crockery
And half-eaten charred jackrabbit.
It passes close by your raving,
Salvation Army mother, your absent father,
Your reprobate, drink-sponging brother,

And flies out the rafter window, back into your night.

Forgetting the deer of long ago, your perfect eyes trained now on this
Black dream, you let loose with a tightly packed round
And blast it out of the sky.

Of course you leave the carcass there.

Closing Salvo

We were linked by ten years of attack on attack.
I knew your appetite for doling out and taking abuse,
So news of your early death delivered a short spasm of grief –
But no big surprise.

We called you Squirrel because you ran like one:
Hopping around the bases on your toes.
You hated the nicknames,
Came back with fists and feet.

One day I peeled off my fear, fought back.
Soon our bus stop skirmishes drew crowds.
Once, bloody shirts ripped off, we rolled into a yard.
You gouged at my eyes; a housewife hosed us down like dogs.

The last time our staggers crossed
Was at the high school graduation party
Near a midnight pasture bonfire.
We laughed when we saw each other
Drinking keg beer out of plastic pitchers.

We talked for a while and refilled each other's drinks.
After that, everything was OK,

Except that I walked around for years
With that pitcher in my hand until it became too heavy
And foamed up all over my life.

So, Adrian – Squirrel – the obit read that you died in
   Hollywood, Florida.
There wasn't much more.
And in reading it, I thought I'd call your home phone,
See if the answering machine was still connected.
I wanted to hear what you sounded like.
But the operator said there was no listing in your name.

We're The Del Crandalls, Parts II and III
(A Four-Part, Ten-Year Special Commemorative Set.
Collect All Four!)

II.

Genius melodist, brutal friend, you told me
 — *I'll be glad when this winter's over.*
Everything I touch shocks me. I'm like some giant Ray-o-Vac.

Tonight you will plug into your Marshall and sad, electronic birds
    will fly from the poles of your hands.

III.

Hey: compatriot, wise, neurotic, therapy-
Riddled companion of Jesus, Colossus
At failing jobs and love, set your kit up here.
Your rhythms will soothe the beatless, feed the
Rage, bark commands to the guitars.

When you stop, we'll all be naked. Start playing again, quick.

You Have Killed Sweet Love's Groovy Stance

Let's be adults about this, my little metaphor for the heather,
On the off chance that we'll not return to that sad state.
Let us kiss away for good the off-kilter fire-eating tight wire walker
    that is us.
We should not be inclined toward the moronic, sweet nymph of
    the twilight, &c. . . .
It's a good bet that this thing has attained its logical denouement,
    & so forth.
I.e., arcane *Bacchus* has floated by, raising his glass
In love's soft refrain.

Splendid human cuspidor of mine, my spaghetti will continue to be yours,
My heart continues to explode in rhapsodic refrains, as it were.
O! Walking verse-form (as you will, one would hope, continue to be),
Warmer of all heart-cockles, lust-giver of the spring dew,
I now the following notice advance:
You have killed sweet love's groovy stance.

To the homeboy who stole my car stereo with tape 3, side 2 from "A Century of Recorded Poetry" still in it (on the occasion of Richard Eberhart's 99th birthday)

and stole my child's car seat, as well: Greetings. Did you hop to the nearest hock shop, dump the radio, give the car seat to your old lady to shut her up? Or maybe you held on to the radio. You should have. You worked harder for it than I did. All I had to do to earn that money was push paper across my desk for a few days, make a few phone calls that meant nothing, look serious when I had to. When I turned the money over for that factory-installed, clean new Blaupunkt Wolfsburg Edition AM/FM stereo with the high-end tape player with auto-reverse and Dolby, I felt like I was the one who stole it. You earned it: stayed out all night in the cold, looked over your shoulder for cops, put your ass in front of wild strangers to jack them out of dope and cash, tried to sleep on your old lady's couch while her kids screamed and she forced her big ass down on you for sex again while you're coming down from a sorry-ass paint high: *You got the car seat, I got no money, leave me ALONE, you're crazy. At least you didn't have to go my bail this time.* That's a hard working man. Keep that superfine car stereo with the happening low-end, connect it up into your low rider, fiddle with the Ultra Bass control, push the On button, sit back. You will hear Richard Eberhart continuing with his poem, "The Groundhog," from 1939. That's what I was listening to when I shut the car off and went inside for the night:

. . . Inspecting close maggots' might
And seething cauldron of his being,
Half with loathing, half with a strange love,
I poked him with an angry stick. . . .

If your *Chollo* was kickin' it next to you when Richard Eberhart's voice shook your barrio, you would open your mouth wide, make a loud sound, rip the motherfucker out, laugh, crush the tape with your heel. But you are alone. You don't know all the words of this crazy talk, but his flow is so old school. You will get back to your Salsa and Meringue and Florida hardcore rap later on:

. . . The sap gone out of the groundhog,
But the bony sodden hulk remained

But the year had lost its meaning, . . .

You listen over and over. Later you hold the paper bag with the gold paint to your mouth and huff hard. Everything goes away. Your barrio, your tunes, your girlfriend, your old lady back home with the kids. Except for the sapless groundhog that has collected his spine and his ribs and his guts back up and has been sloughing around in your head. He stops, spreads out a deck of mystery cards. You take one. He tells you that this card means that Richard Eberhart likes chicks with big ass too. You turn, face west, spill your own words down the aqueduct, your striking and erudite basso profundo stretching like solemn columns of doom across boundless valleys. Over rusted Maytags. Over parted-out car hulks, and your checkerboard of surface streets, to the sea.

A Real Homey Tragedy

It certainly was a crying shame.
The wind in the willows tipped the weathervane.
A full week's pay or more went into that vane –
It was a nice weathervane; perhaps the best.

It pointed to the corn in the summer and the goose in the fall.
In the winter it would come in and point down the hall.

And old Jud Slaughterhead denied any part in the tipping,
Even though someone saw him last night behind a bough,
Even though he sounds a lot like the new cow.

I saw him once in our lower forty-two
Where the tree line falls at the edge of sight.
A hare turned back. But he was gone in the night.

People talk when a shoulder disdains the plough
And wheat goes fallow, exposing the husk.
When the barn swallow's flat eye turns cold at dusk.

The worst part was that it killed Auntie Nell.
It killed Auntie Nell when it fell, when it fell.

And it came as a shock to me and my brother
When we found her on her back
With "East" on one bosom and "West" on the other.

Raymond, Maine

In the tintype, Captain Harmon
Stands astern in his little side-wheel steamboat.
His crew surrounds him on the covered promenade deck.
The passengers,
Women in long dresses, men in straw hats,
Squint in the afternoon sun,
The great Sebago stretching out before them like their lives.

On that day, death for them is something still to happen –
Corporeal, like the town was on the morning it first
Stretched out before our common ancestor, James Harmon,
Who paddled up the Presumpscot River,
Came ashore at what would be Sebago Pond.

It is afternoon. My great-great-grandfather stands.
Light sharpens the roofs of houses in the village.
Dashes of clouds blow wildly about.

I will return to Raymond at the arrival of winter,
Watch the lake spread out against the fields
For miles, snow on the ground.
Light will sharpen the roof of my memory

As I steal away in a dugout canoe
From the head of Kettle Cove and
Paddle north to the mouth of the Jordan River,
Where I attack, and enter my city.

Resurrection of the Packard Tribe

The boy, his head a space of darkening dreams,
Sits behind the wheel in the hulk of a 1936 Packard C-120,
Abandoned deep in the woods by the Indian burial mounds.

It has rotted and rusted down to a basket-case. He smells the baking rust
Of the floppy hood, stares at what's left of the straight-8 engine block.
Behind him he hears the brook move over mossy stones.
He imagines the car, new, taking a family to distant cities on rainy nights:
Topeka. Plattsburgh. Leominster.
How did it come to die here, with the Indians?

His hands know all her parts. Her pistons are his pistons.
Her graves are his graves.
He wonders who the last people were to care
About each Nipmuc buried here, this car.

Suppertime, he makes the long trek home down the old tractor path.
Later, just before the day cranks over and dies,
From his bedroom window he sees
Some Indians rise up, enter the Packard and depart.

Deal to the Class—

   – After Dickinson

Deal to the Class—
Austin odds-a-great—
His Queen set the seal—Tripped on the "Mount"—
What hand—so fumbling—
Slipped on the Font?

Susan slipped sober—'tis Greatly known—
And shines a great "Wheel"—her Face—
On My Lawn—

Returns

1.

Soon the recurring dream will return me to that lonely kingdom of
     overpasses,
And I'll stand in the breakdown lane of the Unknown Highway again.
Seasons change in matters of instants, but I only see the changes. I won't
     feel them.
Coffee cups spill out across the tough median grasses.
Sustained cornet blasts arise in the distance
Over hills black with growth.

Birds will be present overhead.
Stacked highways arch into and around the city I never quite enter.
Ruined cement columns present a banal acropolis.
The tar on the oak guardrails smells like museum ships.
I have been here for as long as I can remember.
A psychic studied a picture of my daughter a few years ago
And looked up:

 — *Where did you go? She misses her father terribly.*

Squinting at me, she said:

 — *Did you die?*

2.

On the day I left Ireland I sat in the train station at New Ross.
Andrew whispered *That old lady is staring at you.*

 — *My God*, she said, *who are your people?*
You're the spirit and image of my dead husband.

I told her I was American, and I was heading home that afternoon.

— Please don't think I'm rude, but do you mind if I look at you some before you go?
I'm just a 77 year old woman who lost her husband many years ago.
Are you sure you're not him? She laughed, wiped away a tear.

I tried to make small talk, but could see that I'd opened up
Some fresh chapter of mourning for her,
And my stupid conversation wasn't going to change that.

— Your friend looks like an American. But you, you're Irish.

She saw me out to the train, kissed my cheek, waved.
As we pulled out of the station she sang out:
— Good-bye, my love!

— That your grandmother? the man next to me asked.

No, I replied.

But I suddenly remembered that just the day before,
Walking down a street in Rosslaire Harbor,
I was hit with the realization that I had been
Looking for a doorknob that fit my hand.

Traits: Sixteen Stones in a Field

Peer down the mossy well of this old snapshot, this life:
Look at your face. It's a country.
You swim through the ruined house still,
Through our plain pilgrim faces, over the little stone crosses
Singing low songs of age, farm accident, drowning,
The croup, famine-rot-in-a-bog.

At the ancient and sick end of your life
I was your February, always presaging the arrival of rain.
The lone skater who traced frozen worlds over worlds of pond-sleep
While darkness threatened the woods.
I was your leaden dream, the one that refused to lift off.
The grave of every hope.

Now I try to be April to my own daughter
Who bears the shape of your moods and wears your face so perfectly
As she draws her tiny paper moon and
Tells me *When the sky cries, we all will cry*
On this, a happy day, and she's right:
The slate-gray sky is open and near birdless.
(But the birds in my daughter's bones
Cry with happiness under the moon of her moods.)

I framed your picture a year ago.
Your beauty hangs gaily over the street.
Limps on tired trestles home.
Drives the thunder deeper.
Calls your names in order.

PART III

Fall

We come down our road charged
With a hard energy. The words are jailed
Up in the spaces of our minds, except for
The odd ones that escape the pressure of our heads
In our way, on our road, past the tire trucks
And the parked school buses. Another group
Is talking sideways, eyes on us:
The one with the green shirt makes his remark
Straight out this time, so we cross the street.

The screwdriver gulped from your Mason jar
Tells you to seek out the big one. You wait for him to smile,
Drive your fist into his grin like a pile driver.
The one behind him jumps you. His buddy,
Third man in, shoves a boot into your balls
As the groups converge, wild. Ecstasies –
Sometimes you just want to get beaten.

The years go by. You might lose your job.
Your kid gets sick. Your liver is half shot, or maybe
Your marriage turns bad. You go back to your road,
But the tire trucks are gone, a 7-11
Has gone up in the lot where they were kept.
If you'd met someone new,
You would want her there, with you.

You look down into an oily puddle, carnival mirror Narcissus,
And blink the words *how are you*
To the jail you see before you.
On the day you meet yourself,
Your lady never arrives in blue jeans and sweater.

And just like that you come up with nothing to pound,
no one to jump you.

Fort Nathan Hale Death Stanzas
– For Billy, Dead at 32

*There are such unfortunates. They seem to have been born
that way. Their chances are less than average.*

– From *The Big Book of Alcoholics Anonymous*

And now, what have we to show for your life –
A few roofs patched up,
New black spread on the odd driveway,
A few Marlboro butts moldering by the back door.
A gravesite, sealed granite.

In the end, you just couldn't make all the pieces fit.
The rosary wrapped around the hand I shook
Just a few days before almost hides sins
Committed before your father was born.

You were too close to danger.
When the police got there it was too late.
She was a crazed junkie, and she put your life
Out like a cigarette.

Go home, faithful servant, and jump blindly through the cosmos.
It was never like you to indulge in common sense.

Winter Piss, Outside the Shock-Ward

The old bum's heart sputters to the edge of giving out.
Another Arctic blast whips that hot
Bucket of smoke into a fiery dance: He smiles.
The canvas wrapped around his raw mitts burns.

He shifts his weight,
Refuses to communicate
With the pantheon of laughing gods
Whose heads now appear in balls of flame.

He fumbles with his fly, sees
Steaming liquid that branches
In lines, like beasts charging,
Two and by two,
Away from him, to safety.

He looks at what's left of his cigarette
And tosses it up at what's left of the world.

Still Life with Marriage Counselor

On the calendar there is an albatross. Evening is falling. I sense that
    the bird is hungry.
So am I. I hear the marriage counselor say:

Every day is the same for Muhammed Ali. He wakes up at seven o'clock,
Puts his clothes on in the same preordained pattern:
Underwear first, pants, shirt, socks, shoes.

Fold and unfold. Fold and unfold.

He grunts quietly, in slow croaking rhythms: only he knows the code.
Life and death are the same for Ali –
He will not break the ritual –
He could not even break the ritual
To go see Cosell in the hospital
On the day the old man bleated out his name one last time,
Cancer tearing into his neck.

Life today is repetition and structure for Cassius Clay:
The tired magic tricks (always the same, done in the same way,
    in the same order),
The way he has of turning his whole body when just a turn
    of the neck would do,
The trips to the doctors. He'll disappear into the john for an hour.

He'll fold into the john for an hour, and then unfold.
Folding and unfolding, like a lilac, past wide seas and time.
He has this dream, he told someone, that when he dies,
His head will join those big stone ones out on Easter Island.

We fold ourselves with clumsy hands.
We argue again over stupid things.
We try to out-scream and out-clever each other.

The marriage counselor drones on in Cosellian tones.
I will not visit him on his hospital gurney.

Out on Easter Island an albatross floats over the stone heads,
    waits for The Champ.

Symphony for Pond Mud, Several Gifted Frogs, and the Death of the Last Survivor of the Spanish Inquisition

Slick green dancers, furtive, line up pond side,
Stretched on a hummock of wide earth
Beneath a rock vestibule spanning the sky
Of frog country. Formalities aside,
The frogs are really pretty nice –

Eyes bulbous and sad, they raise
Their pitch in arrays of symphonic after-tones.
The depths sing in low, alien cadences.

One resembles not so much J. Edgar Hoover
As Lillian Gish. Her beauty creates quite a
Stir in these parts. Her lips swim dark in her pale ocean of face.

The rocks take on human outlines as the
Mettle of knighthood corrodes by the beach.

A Dinner Bell Unanswered

And they finally drudged
The big body
Of J. D. Spiller up from the muck

And soon it was news
All over Raymond Village:
The men were saying
They found Spiller
Face down in the bog.

And his limbs held stiff
And stubborn
Down, down, down on the bottom
Unyielding like axe handles

And they had to pry him
Face down like a steeped bull from the mud

And they finally pulled the hatless corpse
Of Spiller out of the bog,

And it took two plough horses
And several good neighbors
To lug him from the mud

And they heaved him muddy
Onto the bank like a sack.

And from the hill, the terrible unanswered
Dinner bell –

St. Brigid and the Gull Who Would Be a Man

> *. . . a soul may make history and move the world, though leaving little to tell concerning its passage through this world. Our Lady's own life on earth was almost wholly hidden. . . . [There is] an old fable in which Brigid is supposed to have been nurse to the Infant Jesus.*
>
> – Saint Brigid: The Mary of the Gael

You take flight in the morning
Over the rounded stones of Durrow's Ledge,
Disrobe, wade out. The tired head
Of a saint

Lies face up off the strand, in a soft spread
Of curls lapping the Irish Sea.
Up the Derry coast, the hag with a stick
Walks the promontory in circles,

Muttering about time
And the end of all things.
If she notices your nude grace
She might not mention it

To the curlews and gulls
Dipping and calling. One bird
Knows the story about you nursing
The Child Jesus,

And, as your aquatic breasts bob,
Says to you in a voice as ordinary as my own:
If I were a man, I would lie on you
And touch palm to palm.

I would twin your fingers with mine.
I would die just to touch my mouth to your watery leg.
To run my finger over your pelvic bone.
To slide the secret bush apart.

TV Baby

He stayed in last prime-time
Witnessing his own birth:
A big, happy nocturne
Of cheese balls and chain saws

"The wilderness was wild,
Surmised scurrilous Sal
"But now I'm home –
Not alone, quite well-known."

He burped his way through a half-keg of suds
And just before kissing the carpet
He said:
"I can't watch that show again!
"I can't watch that show again!
"Somebody lose me that fabulous womb!
"Make way for the sunlight that's filling this room!"

Someone cut the cord with a big, cheesy knife
His mother, the giant, bled and came down
Smothering the knife
(Now a giant cheese-covered scythe)
With a garageful of flesh only barely alive
And a tongue that could taste what
Her child was worth
As he stayed in last prime-time
Just watching his birth.

The Crows

August, driving down I-91 a week before my thirty-ninth birthday.
I push the tape into the cassette player:
"An Anthology of Poets Reading Their Poems."

It begins with the impossible –
Whitman reading a bit of his "America,"
Recorded by Edison himself on a wax cylinder in 1892.

This voice – vaulting from so deep in the graveyard
That it might be the rattling voice of Christ himself –
Gives up words of felled oak
Hard and perfectly hewn,
Dried and stacked out of the weather
In a forgotten shed too far from town.

The ghost voice is punctuated
With the rhythmic whoosh of an imperfection
In the wax, with a regularity like rain
Driving back and forth across slates.

Thirty miles later, James Wright reads as the sky leadens.
Crows raise and flatten wing tips over a billboard.
Their black forms settle into iambs and trochees.

This Skull Once Had a Tongue

My fight with the sea of sleep blasts street side.
Wind sweeps by in flourishes of white and leaves.

But for you, this world of sleep is gone:
Your mind has taken root at the edges of a cleaner place,
Your streets buried under the slush you trudged.
Your office slouches vacant through dismal afternoons.
Dusty logic avoids even the living spiders
Who, come spring, will poke about the churchyard and
Camp in the marrow of your eye sockets.

Reason courses away in pointed boots, as
From under the round tower,
Something shifts
The positions of the stars.

THE DEL CRANDALLS

Song Lyrics

To listen to the following songs, visit GreatHornedPublishing.com and follow the link for "The Del Crandalls."

Tex

Someone drove the car around . . . and Tex brought the knives.

– Former Manson Family member Patricia "Katie" Krenwinkel in jailhouse interview with Diane Sawyer

It was one of those mornings when the money's all gone
I was feeling as wild as a whip
Made breakfast for the boys, and then I went on a trip

But I never left the ranch
And then it was night
Someone drove the car around, and Tex brought the knives.

Early in the morning, Clem had the Longhorn
Firing away at some cans
Satan rising up, my baby turning handstands

She said now don't be afraid
You should listen to your wife
The moon rattled like candy and Tex brought the knives.

Been wasting days
Feeling so blue
I'm so strung out
In love with you

Right on the money, but the money's all gone
And I'm feeling kind of sick – do you still say you're sorry
When the man in the moon becomes the life of the party?

———

A bus load of wise men
Breaking out in hives
Charlie kept on smilin', and Tex brought the knives.

Been wasting days
Feeling so blue
I'm so strung out
In love with you

Katie, Leslie, Sadie, Linda: Tex brought the knives.

Common Man

His boss didn't understand him
And his girl was high on smack
So he drove downtown in his Dyna-Flow
And he ain't coming back

Cruising past the windows:
Caldor's, Woolworth's, Sears
He stops on in to Johnnie B's
For fifty-seven *pots* of beer

This is the story of a common man
My life is so complete –
Ketchup-stained turtleneck, train-conductor's cap
Tractor pull front-row seat
This is the story of a common man
His name is Napkin Ned – or so I read.

His last day in the restaurant
They threw his last check on the floor
He'd trash that place in two seconds flat
If they called him "Napkin Ned" once more

But now he's got a job at Woolworth's
He's found a drug-free bride
And he spends his days making chocolate malts
With an extra thing of malt on the side

This is the story of a common man. . . .

His boss didn't understand him
His girl was high on smack
It's such a happy day
With all the children singing

This is the story of a common man. . . .

Two Days of Rain

All day long my baby keeps on rocking me
The seventh-inning stretch, please please please
Quarter-tank of gas and nothing much to talk about
Driving through the tunnel listening to the Bee Gees

She says "Nothing can replace what we had,
Nothing can make good out of bad,
What about the tears that we shed?"

Five o'clock news and we start a little argument
I don't like Don Johnson and I don't like Mister T
My neck is getting tense 'cause I see that you're enjoying them
And all the other drug addicts you watch on your TV

She says "Nothing can replace what we had,
Nothing can make good out of bad,
What about the tears that we shed?"

Two days of rain
Better than the Cokes we shared
Better than the love we had
Better than all that, I swear

Then one night, my baby had a crazy dream
We raised Carl Hubbell with a bell and cup –
She said "Wake up, dead man, the devil's in the house tonight –
Wake up dead man, wake up, wake up"

And then she says "Nothing can replace what we had . . ."

Rye Beach Roustabouts

It's cold outside, he found a place to hide
In the corner where the sun never shines
Sammy looks around, puts one ear to the ground
Someone lifts him up and says "Who are those guys?"

Who are those guys? We are the Rye Beach Roustabouts.

Sleep on, sister, walked around in a fog and I missed her
Now no doctor's smart enough to shape me up
Disconnect my phone, tell the carnival crowd to go it alone
I forgot to duck, but I won't forget your eyes

Who are those guys? We are the Rye Beach Roustabouts.

When it all comes down, it's the death of your class clown
Have some fries and hear my stupid elegy
No muss, no fuss; you sleep in the road, you might get hit by a bus
The charade is up and you're hung out to dry

Who are those guys? We are the Rye Beach Roustabouts.

Our Town

Thornton Wilder never wrote about our town
It's wild, so you might want to turn around

Death metal plays by the water
It's a cold day here without you
Got your scholars, got your vandals
Teachers still get stoned and wear sandals

I'm a stand-up guy in a sitting-duck town
Feeling like a fly on an Afghan Hound
Weather's getting hotter
Thought I felt a swatter
What's the litmus test today?
Don't need no Berlitz tapes to say

Farewell, my astonishing beauty –
So long, so long, so long.

I've looked under every stone
Still can't tell just where the ants are going
And you, my love, don't look like that
In your Jackie-O gloves and your pillbox hat
I'll stay on the straight and narrow
I will ape Clarence Darrow

But if you ever find the reason
To fold in the last weeks of the season
Then sing with us, ye Cherubim
Sing with us, Gene Sarazen

All the angels seize the day,
All my troubles gone away.

Farewell, my astonishing beauty –
So long, so long, so long.

Man Ray

Lately you've been thinking way too much
You're looking way too thin
The morning comes crashing down to the ground
We're trying to draw you in

She likes Man Ray; she says it's an affair of the heart.

The Alameda swimming pool
Look what Joe's done now –
We're one man short on the Wing-T
And she says I seem too highbrow, but

She likes Man Ray; she says it's an affair of the heart.

Ginger Snaps

Ginger wore a halo in the passion plays last year
Then her head grew larger and it cut into her ear
Ginger never kisses me, we just get drunk all the time
She talks about her paintings and how all the world's sublime
But I see through the colors in her eyes
When Ginger Snaps

Ginger was an athlete like Dennis "Oil Can" Boyd
Then she got asthma, now it's sports she must avoid
Ginger says I'm beautiful we get drunk all the time
She talks about her paintings and how poetry should rhyme
But I see through the colors in her eyes
When Ginger Snaps

Ginger wants to be an actress but the halos cut her head
She wants to be an athlete but she barely moves instead
One day I will kiss her in the mist down by the pier
And then we'll move through the shadows like two legs on Fred Astaire

ACKNOWLEDGMENTS

The author wishes to thank Vivian Shipley, Jeff Mock, and Charles Fort for their wisdom, guidance, and editorial suggestions; Ron Jost for his belief in my writing, deft editorial hand, enthusiasm, and patience with missed deadlines; and Matt Smith for his terrific proofreading skills.

Heartfelt thanks and gratitude are also extended to Barry Gelston, Aleta Truebig, Stacy Vocacek, Andrew Narciso, Ron Saleh, and Greg Antonini for being kind and encouraging along the way, and to GL and CAZ, who cause spontaneous poetry wherever they go.

Most of all, I would be remiss in not attributing and dedicating the poems "Memoirs of an Aesthete" and "At Versace's" to James Estarellas, who wrote the original versions as a teenager. Many years after the fact, after trying unsuccessfully to find him and get the originals, I have attempted to re-create his work from memory and, as such things go, have likely done violence to them by forgetting parts and/or filling in the blanks (and adding titles). The resulting amalgams, poor copies as they are, will hopefully broadcast his talents to someone who appreciates them like I do.

ABOUT THE AUTHOR

Rich Bowering's poems have appeared in *Caduceus* and *Folio Art & Literary Magazine*. While studying for his M.A., he was the first winner of the Southern Connecticut State University E.D.G.E. (English Department Graduate Ensemble) poetry contest, and took first place in the 2003 Folio graduate student poetry contest. His poem "And Then the Song Conjured Up Your Soft White Shoulders All Over Again" won the 2011 Valentine's Day Love Poem Contest sponsored by WCLV Classical FM. He was the lead singer for The Del Crandalls. A native of Connecticut, he lives in Cleveland.

Contact the author at rich_bowering@hotmail.com.